MW01277444

LO QUE VEO/ WHAT I SEE

By Alex Appleby

Traducción al español: Christina Green

Gareth Stevens
PUBLISHING

Please visit our website, www.garethstevens.com. For a free color catalog of all our high-quality books, call toll free 1-800-542-2595 or fax 1-877-542-2596.

Library of Congress Cataloging-in-Publication Data

Appleby, Alex.
What I see = Lo que veo / by Alex Appleby.
p. cm. — (My five senses = Mis cinco sentidos)
Parallel title: Mis cinco sentidos
In English and Spanish.
Includes index.
ISBN 978-1-4824-0870-6 (library binding)
1. Vision — Juvenile literature. 2. Senses and sensation — Juvenile literature. I. Appleby, Alex. II. Title.
QP475.7 A66 2015
612.8—d23

First Edition

Published in 2015 by
Gareth Stevens Publishing
111 East 14th Street, Suite 349
New York, NY 10003

Editor: Ryan Nagelhout
Designer: Andrea Davison-Bartolotta
Spanish Translation: Christina Green

Photo credits: Cover, p. 1 Blend Images/Thinkstock; p. 5 DigitalFabiani/Shutterstock.com; p. 7 Andrey Ospishchev/Hemera/Thinkstock; p. 9 JessieEldora/iStock/Thinkstock; p. 11 Yobro10/iStock/Thinkstock; p. 13 Ryan McVay/The Image Bank/Getty Images; p. 15 (classroom) Digital Light Source/UIG via Getty Images; p. 15 (snake) mmpile/iStock/Thinkstock; p. 15 (wood chips) Sergii Moskaliuk/Hemera/Thinkstock; p. 17 andresr/E+/ Getty Images; p. 19 tristan tan/Shutterstock.com; pp. 21, 24 (hippo) tratong/Shutterstock.com; pp. 23, 24 (moon) Suppakij1017/Shutterstock.com.

Printed in the United States of America

CPSIA compliance information: Batch #CS15GS: For further information contact Gareth Stevens, New York, New York at 1-800-542-2595.

Contenido

Ver cosas 4

Mostrar y contar 12

El zoológico. 18

Palabras que debes saber 24

Índice 24

- -

Contents

Seeing Things .4

Show-and-Tell .12

The Zoo. 18

Words to Know 24

Index. 24

Veo con los ojos.

I see with my eyes.

El sol brilla mucho.

The sun is very bright.

7

Veo un autobús escolar.
Es amarillo.

I see a school bus.
It is yellow.

8

SCHOOL BUS

Voy a la escuela.
Veo a mis amigos.

I go to school.
I see my friends.

Podemos mostrar
y compartir cosas.
Yo enseño mi
nuevo juguete.

We have show-and-tell.
I show people
my new toy.

13 Colonies in early America

¡Veo una serpiente!
Tiene muchas rayas.

I see a snake!
It has many stripes.

15

Después de la clase
veo a mi papá.

I see my dad
after school.

Me lleva al zoológico.

He takes me to the zoo.

Veo muchos animales.
Incluso veo
un hipopótamo.

I see lots of animals.
I even see a hippo.

21

¡Veo la Luna!
Está en el cielo
de noche.

I see the moon!
It is in the sky at night.

23

Palabras que debes saber/ Words to Know

(el) hipopótamo/
hippo

(la) Luna/
moon

Índice / Index

hipopótamo/hippo 20

Luna/moon 22

mostrar y compartir/
show-and-tell 12

ojos/eyes 4